PLENTY OF EXITS

PLENTY OF EXITS

NEW AND SELECTED POEMS

Martin Tucker

CONFRONTATION PRESS
Long Island University • Brookville, New York

None of the incidents, situations, or plot devices in the narrative poems in this book is to be taken as factual or (auto)biographical. I have observed the customs of fiction in drawing my points.

Some of these poems have appeared in earlier form in the magazines *Boulevard, Confrontation, Home Planet News ,LIPS, Potpourri, helicon, Northern Centinel, New York Times*, and in the volumes of poetry by Martin Tucker, *Homes of Locks and Mysteries; Attention Spans;* and *While There Is Time*, and in the anthology, *Fathers*, edited by David and Judy Ray.

Poems that are dated (bottom line) have been selected from previous book publication or are notated to suggest an earlier time.

Library of Congress Control Number: 2008935576
ISBN 978-0-913057-54-4

Cover art: Detail of a photo by R.M. Ross
Cover design and book design by John Beck

Printed in the United States of America
First printing: November 2008

Confrontation Press
Long Island University
Brookville, N.Y. 11548-1300

For Number 13, with love

and again to Lee

Contents

Life Works

Death Works

Natural Works

Cuba Poem

Martin Tucker

D. H. Melhem

Martin Tucker's fourth collection, *Plenty of Exits: New and Selected Poems*, holds a treasure of surprises. Three new introductory poems, "How Being in Love in a Cold Clime Changes a Man's Life," "The Man Who Peed on the Williamsburg Bridge On a Warm Wednesday Afternoon," and "The Gift of the Magi, Or, An Old Kind of Romance," audaciously tipped in, are deliberately set. They provide clues to a new element of his work: a liberated honesty about topics that are often taboo, confessional matters regarding personal foibles and sex. While we delight in welcoming again pieces we've admired in previous volumes of his, the ample offering of new poems gives a major indication of growth and of empowering new directions.

What amazes in this work is how far the poet continues to advance from a point of full maturity in his life and art, and how generously he includes us in the process. His range includes family, its gifts and losses, animals, art, literature, travel, and specific poets like Yeats, D.H. Lawrence, and Wallace Stevens. The gemlike wit is there, epigrams and puns that radiate throughout the language, along with the wisdom of memorable lines like "Those years never lived never die" and "I cannot forget what is impossible for me to remember" (from "The Missing Father").

Tucker concludes with "Ten Days in Cuba," one of the most powerful works in his oeuvre. Among the experiences culled from his journeys, this poem is a major gem. It appears as a journal sequence of free verse and prose poems about his trip to the island in 2001. Tucker's vivid account, itself a useful primer on the country and its hospitable citizens, contains a starkly indelible reflection on Che Guevara. The poet images the Cuban being tortured on a table while he himself is lying in comfort on a similar table enjoying a massage. This stunning juxtaposition pulls the reader toward confronting the cruelties of current political affairs. It does so with a seeming casualness that emphasizes the obscenity of today's all-too-common usage of "interrogation techniques."

In the last poem of Tucker's previous book he asks, "How Far Does a Poem Have to Go?" and concludes, musing aloud, "How far do I want to go? How deep?" *Plenty of Exits* gives his answer. It lies beyond boundaries. Sturdily, within the strict yet limitless parameters of art, it beckons affirmatively and excitingly to the future, at (or from) whatever stage the reader may be contemplating it.

OPENINGS /
CLOSINGS /
BY CHOICE

How Being in Love in a Cold Clime
Changes a Man's Life

Sweet flannel seeps into the cool air unseen.
The skin tastes a hundred blankets of warm snow.
Trees bloom in the dressing room.

The Man Who Peed On the Williamsburg Bridge
On a Warm Wednesday Afternoon

It was an urgent matter,
something not to be dismissed
without venting of expression —
A stream of pure tension.

Below skies of blue clarity
I unleashed my holdings.
They sailed forth into the winds of chance,
taking equal sides against the throngs nearby.

Historians will say it was an insignificant foray.
Yet curiously the armor of cars thrust forward,
the workers on the construction site fell back,
and, I believe, caissons moved into the city briskly.

Martin Tucker

The Gift of the Magi,
Or, An Old Kind of Romance

1.
He lay in the waiting dark
lying across white sheets of bed
worried he would be lying to her
this first night of their love-making.

He had a problem—the problem big,
the penis small, ripe in undersize,
he could tell her it was no matter,
she might not agree about the assessment.

It was a moment he had to face.
His hopes high to rise to the occasion.

2.
She thought him a marvel.
She had given up marvels.
They had met at a dinner party.
She could not believe he came alone.

When he phoned her, his voice tentative,
she seized on his invitation.
That first night it was dinner
and a play after. No need for worries.

She knew men desired sex, needed arms
to thrust battle cries. Games they called love.

3.
He would not tell her his history.
That was a pastime when he needed excuses.
He would tell her another kind of story,
How an operation succeeded but ended in boundaries.

Besides, his will might turn round the situation.
Blood-red veins might prick him to the quick.
If he kept his mind on his vision
they might ascend to showering appetites.

He wanted to please her, of that he was sure.
Later he would worry about her wanting more.

4.
How could she forget that men would not relent,
that their need was for show as well as score.
He was different but the same. She wanted to please him.
She did not want to lose by skirting her legs.

The man before the man waiting for her
had shown her what men do when they are denied.
He had ripped her dress, held her arms down
till he depleted his source.

How could she tell her new lover her place was sealed?
And worse, she felt nothing, only distaste.

Martin Tucker

5.
He lay waiting for her in the waiting dark,
anticipating excuses he would employ.
The prostate operation, the heart condition —
tissues and shields for things he would not admit.

He cared for her. Surely she knew that.
Yet he was coy for fear she would detect
that indifference he could not disguise,
the wanting of passion stepping from behind.

No, he said, she did not know of it.
He had tonight to correct past errors.

6.
It was months ago she went to her doctor
who soothed the pain. Medicine brought
a bodily peace but left a warring mind.
At sixty she had been date-raped.

He was a gentleman from up North,
a friend of a friend who wanted to comfort
the new widow. The gentleman took her to the best inn —
a martini, a bottle of champagne and no diversion of soul.

At the door he pushed the latch away,
entered her bedroom, commanding his rites.

7.
What would she tell him, he wondered,
she was taking so long. Perhaps she would
whisper the words he most wanted to hear.
"It doesn't matter." Which of course it did.

It mattered to him that he cared,
that age and history were working against him,
that his Casanova air, his charm with women,
would deter her from understanding his kind of passion.

He played with himself. The game was not up.
He wanted her, no matter the condition.

8.
It wasn't only the rape, she knew.
She had tired of sex. That was the cause of the rape.
She had flirted, she had doubled her winks,
He had mistaken her lashes for serious intentions.

She pulled on her flannel gown, a flag of plain
to announce resistance to border crossings.
She wanted sexless fidelity,
an affectionate camp where beds were debunked.

Would he understand?
She opened the door to tell him her story.

                                        Martin Tucker

9.
How plain the nightgown, he thought. Like a nun,
Or a shorn Jewish bride. And the hesitation climbing into bed.
He touched her shoulder, ran his hand down her arm,
Kissed her body as she lay shaking.

She was with him and beyond him,
a bird fluttering in his embrace.
He would bring her to fruition
in the room's awe of silence.

"I must tell you something," she cried,
and he knew and did not know the moment was passing..

10.
She told her story, she could not keep from sobbing,
She fought her tremors, then took a rein of defense.
"It doesn't matter," she said. "Not to me.
But to you, you must decide if it matters."

She waited. She had waited for days to tell him,
waiting for the proper moment,
hoping to deter the crush of revelation
she was sure would ambush their traffic.

She touched his leg, ran her fingers across its hairs.
"I love your body," she said, "lying next to mine."

11.
"I have a story too," he replied. "I hadn't planned on telling it."
"Please," she begged, "tell me yours.
Mine is one disappoints you, doesn't it?
You won't leave me, will you?"

"Darling," he whispered, kissing each part of her body,
down to the center of where it all begins,
"darling, I can't enter or hurt you,
only love you in a way my fashion."

The crossings of his life, the path she would provide
Collided in flanks harnessed to this moment.

12.
He told his story, the one he had promised not to tell,
Of his own rape years and years ago,
The older man promising wisdom.
Glamour to take him to another world.

He worshipped the man for years,
Even now, long after, the memory
Persisted, drawing him to lines
He would not draw himself into.

Do you understand, he said. It spoiled everything.
Down there. Now, with age, it doesn't matter.

Martin Tucker

13.
How they laughed, the two of them,
Laughed the whole night through.
The gift they would be giving each other,
Lying, lying in the bedroom.

It was no lie the love they carried
To their warm bodies in the dark room.
"How blest we are," she sang from her breast,
the words flying like stars of light.

He thought of literature's equivalent,
Hemingway's Jake, O'Henry's Magi..

14.
How many different ways to skin an ecstasy,
How many different ways to spin a tale.
There are only so many things one cannot do,
Let's get started on those we can.

Their bedroom heard its share of sighs,
So deep it seemed the walls demanded rebuilding.
Plenty of exits they found for their drives,
Plenty of paths lay waiting for them.

After many harvests of their plenty,
They told their miracle to a choice few.

FAMILY MATTERS

Motherworks: a prose poem

He's late. So what else is new? He's late every time he comes to see me. He tells me, what's the difference? I'm here, aren't I? There is a difference. I worry. He tells me not to worry, I'm 55 years old, he says. As if that stops a mother from worrying.

He looked tired last time he was here. I tried to tell him to stop running so much. Take it easy, I said. You could have a heart attack like anyone else. He didn't listen. He hasn't listened to me since he was 18.

He's a good boy. He takes care of everything so I get the best care. He watches that they cut the grass. It doesn't matter, I tell him. But he goes and complains. I'm paying for it, he says, for the upkeep. I want your surroundings to look good, he tells them.

Sometimes I tell him he does too much for me. How often I've told him he should get married. It's not right not having a family. He's a Jew. We have to keep our people growing. Don't we have enough enemies without cutting off our birthrate? That's when he yelled at me. First time he raised his voice to me. Imagine, a 55-year-old man yelling at his mother. Shut up, he said. All I said was to tell you to get married, have a family, have someone make a nice supper for you, I said.

I hope he's not sick. Last time he looked run-down. Stooped. A belly. He used to be so good-looking, my son. Maybe that's the way Jewish men go. Not his father. His father stayed thin forever. Ran all the time, kept him thin. One night he left me and didn't come back. Must have kept running. My son's made up for him. He's a good boy. He was always a good boy.

Where is he? This time he's really late. I don't like that. Is it so hard for him to understand that?

What's that they're doing? Putting up a headstone next to me. I was supposed to have the place all to myself. My son told me he paid for both of us, to be here. He was thinking of me even though I told him it's not right. You should lie beside your wife. That's when he shouted at me. Again.

It's a marble headstone. Black, like mine. What a coincidence!

It's got his name on it.

Oh, God! I told him to take it easy.

It's not fair.

How did he go? I should have been there.

I hope he didn't suffer.

Will people think I told him to do this? I swear I told him to get married, have a family, lie beside his wife.

I did my best.

What's done is done. I didn't want him to do this, but it's done. You make the best of what comes your way.

I'm glad he's here.

	Martin Tucker

At My Mother's Grave

Because I could not find your grave—
the cemetery computer was down that day—
I stood amid rows of headstones
and shouted your name to the sky.

Perhaps you heard me,
for onlookers raised their heads.
I reigned down blessings on you,
though it was late for things to be said.

As well and as usual, I was late
(you grew used to my habits).
I have some justice on my side:
I cannot depend on traffic.

Sitting here hours later, I like to remember
myself in your garden of stones,
my arms raised upward,
speaking of love deep in my bones.

I think this time you heard me—
a lone man in a forest of sober doors,
unlocking messages not sent before,
and, more, forgiving his flaws.

Over the Hill

This street is colder than the one we were on,
Let's go back to that other one.
She did not notice, or pretended not to,
A wind had come up about us.
Such was her way of holding at bay
That which she meant to deal with later.
I'm not over the hill yet, she said,
Though everyone knew she was.

The hill is gone now, but there are grounds
I must cover in writing this down.

Martin Tucker

Mother: On Dying, Not Death

1.

When I was young I rode the elevated lines
but called it The Subway.
I liked the roar above the flatlands streets,
the view of windows viewing me
4,5,6 storeys about the ground
my mind was travelling on.
I peered into distances beyond
to discover various identities.
(Now I know it was mine I was tendering).
Sometimes there were shades to darken my view
but I saw chinks of light.
(My mother, to my undying youthful shame,
spoke in one breath of Chinese food and Chinese restaurants
as "Chinks."
I recall the word now with a whimper of wrongdoing.)

What goes down in time comes up as memory.
One girl in a room level with our train
waved her hand through an open window.
She was three, I was ten, I thought we'd do that again —
I was heedless of change in my scheduling.

As if real people were not enough,
I wrote a story.
I saw a blind girl beating her heart against a pane of glass,
her body hiding the way to the tunnel of her room,
her hand smiling at the train.

We waved a greeting—
the blind have a way of knowing
which way the arms of friendship are blowing.

Living as I do now in a high rise
and looking out at a window facing me,
I feel so little exists between.
All is airs here,
none of them grasped.

My mother is dying, I yell. Everyone is dying,
someone shouts back.

2.

As a writer I would not sell my mother for a story,
but I would sell a poem to please her,
to buy back what has not been lost,
yet erased for a time
as on a palimpsest
(I have always wanted to use that word,
but was afraid of erasures in my life.)

For too long, unable to bare my love,
I have made her the carrier of my default.
I hear the healers say it is all
in the gestalt of things.
So, into it to get out of it.

The summer I reached across a subway train
to signal love from a window to a blind girl of three
was the time of evening I watched
sleeveless men smiling athletically
from ribbed and lusting bodies
thrust out of windows of heat.

                                        Martin Tucker

I remember my father then:
handsome and muscled, a specimen
any child might idolize,
and I, more than any, possessed him.
But he was nowhere to be seen.
He had left ages before,
I was sure, because I scored
his periodic absences.
Never again would I complain
about anyone's transient exit.

My mother lives. The news is wondrous, yet alloyed.
I have responded badly in the wake of her sleep,
raging with anguish over alarms from wires
stretched waiting for a click, a stirring out of sleep.
I think of things I never told her.
There were things I never told my father.
My life flows from that hole
he left by leaving us.

I want to tell her I forgive her,
though she has refused the first rust of our love.
I want to tell her I forgive my father,
but I hesitate:
their contest has not ended with his death.
I hear her litany seek out a virgin space:
she is telling me of her devotion to my father,
how she travelled three hours a day to Staten Island
from Far Rockaway,
and later to Pilgrim State.
Names that take on hotel auras,
rooms grayer with each medicine day.
She wants someone to take care of her that way.
She wants justice.
Is it too much to ask? she says.
(I see her sitting up in bed.)

I would like to pay her this demanding courtesy,
but such gestures now strangle my heart.
I remember instead for all the reasons in my world
(though I do not yet know the reasons)
how she cried on a park bench
when I had spent hours visiting a friend.
She did not leave the park till dusk,
a danger I was sure to apprehend
when I returned from my unburdened visit.

A neighbor told me of my mother's tears
as if I could dry them.
I tried talking as a message,
but she never heard the words.
There was something between us
she did not want disturbed.

Or a year earlier going to a party on the first floor
of the high-rise built on low-income status—
my mother did not want me to go, or stay late, there,
she warned me of a dire looming affair,
she told me the hostess had been knifed by her lover
and bore the scars on her back.
I said I was opening a door,
not planning to live in the room.
She remained concerned.
I dressed for the occasion as best I could—
stern brooding look and an open black shirt
(the lovers and the knife had been black,
glistening in the hot-tempered room).

I danced with three women, learning steps
I might take to an improper bend.
I was having a glorious puberty time
when the hostess looked at me with lust on her tongue
(I heard the smile of her clicking teeth).

                              Martin Tucker

Behind her I caught the eye of her lover
reaching down to seize a fitting tool of response —
it might have been a drink to slow his spirits
but what I saw was blood spilling over my already wet pants.

I left an astounded party.
Should I be grateful to my mother
for saving me from such an encounter?
Years later, when I was delayed on an errand,
she cried in the lobby of the Astor Hotel.
Though a guard wickedly charged her
with aging the image of that high-class pick-up station,
she would not leave the steps where we had planned to meet.
I see her weeping,
for my being an hour late.

A poem should build down into the ground,
touch root with the most radical seeker.
Death is a waiting,
Nothing more, and more than that,
a knowing.
My mother has given notice of her dying,
a respite in which to regain our berths.
No matter how many trains rumble through their appointed
tunnel,
I know one day I must ride the subway of her death.
I include her in my railing lines
now I must let her go.

—1985

Pieces

It was Halloween night, though I kept forgetting it. Before I
had come to the apartment, I had remembered the holiday
and thought children might come to the door. Then, in the
apartment, moving things, I forgot the date. There were so
many other things to finish up in her domain.

It had been three weeks since she died, and for the past
two weeks I had entered the apartment to "vacate" it. The first
week was easier, for arranging the burial, handling the neces-
sary details, greeting people with their condolences, prevented
the despair I knew would surface in isolation.

My cousin flew in from California, a continent's coast
away, and stayed the first few days. Together we visited the
apartment; together we bought the roach powder and the
"bomb" to disinfect the space. Lee set off the "bomb" as we
escaped from the studio apartment in the housing complex for
a few hours. When we returned, the smell hung in the air. My
eyes and ears ached, my nose felt the strain of a canyon of taut
bone, but I insisted we continue the riddance of her posses-
sions. I could say "riddance" to Lee, even "leaving" and
"departing" and "dying," but "vacating" drove me toward
hysteria. To vacate meant to empty out, and to empty out
meant to leave things behind without a proper storage of
memory. Besides, I did not want to go through her things. It
was not so much what I would find—or worse, what I would
not—as it was acknowledging the fact of her death.

I was not an only child. My mother had given birth to a
daughter before I came into being, but I was a son for whom
every Jewish family prays as a means of procreating salvation.
Ironically, it was my sister who delivered three children and I

                                    Martin Tucker

who gave birth to none. Perhaps that is the reason I remained my mother's favorite, perhaps being my mother's son was the reason I never became a parent. All these years later the questions remain. I did not want revelation now. Indeed, for years, I had accepted the quietus of whatever conditions had been laid down at my birth.

In the weeks before my mother's death I wanted to talk with her, to discover the dating of the bloom of her flowers of love for my father, whom she had scolded and punished with diatribe after he left her and even after he returned to her. After his death she turned him into an icon, telling me what a honorable man he was. I wanted to ask her why she and her daughter had fared so poorly in their familial journeys, why there had been so little love between them. The one time in thirty years I saw my mother spread her arms out to show love for my sister was six years ago when my sister died painfully of cancer. My mother invoked the sobs of missed chances and grew silent again in her reserve.

Now all of them—my father who died of cancer twelve years earlier, my mother, my sister—were gone. I felt survivor's guilt. I think that was the reason I did not want to go through her things. I could bear the grief as long as I pushed everything into an abstract of circumstance.

But now I had to empty her apartment. She had lived in it for fifteen years and had poured so much into living there, for as the years went by she stopped going outside. Her bed and her kitchen table became her companions. And like many older people moving onto another stage of lesser movement, she refused to throw anything away. She was always one for holding on, never knowing when a receipt or a letter might come in handy, but in the past few years she had become obsessive about saving any kind of correspondence. Envelopes could not be discarded because she could employ them as scrap paper. Using something once was not enough.

It was not a question of miserliness or even thrift. It was more, an issue of proving she could keep things in an order of

her choosing. For years she had triumphed in her meals, then
when energy flagged, she gave up any preparation of them. I
arranged for a woman to bring her meals (and the plastic
accompaniments of cutlery so she would not have to wash
anything), but my mother kept taking out her utensils, her
cracked dishes, her scores of glasses she stored in the cup-
boards. For a week I had been packing the glasses, the silver-
ware, the dishes into heavy plastic trash bags and carrying
them into the hall for the super to cart away. I had come in on
my days off from teaching at the university, parked my car in
the garage below the building complex, picked up her infre-
quent mail (always bills from doctors or statements from
Medicare). I worked alone in the cluttered room—the half-
kitchen, the dressing room that fronted the bathroom, and
the large studio room. When the Salvation Army men
arrived at the end of three weeks to take away her furniture,
I considered myself lucky they carted off all the items, for I
heard many times they refused furniture if a missing knob, a
tattered armchair cover, were discovered in their survey. Yet
after I had packed and brought out into the hall some fifty
trash bags, the apartment remained crowded. There was still a
heap of leaving left in the space she had called home for
fifteen years.

What had I thrown away: more than 30 dresses, some new
or never worn, some patched beyond vital wear; five coats, one
her granddaughter bought for me to give to her, a long wool
Saks coat she had worn twice, protesting the style was not right
for her; four other overcoats, all hand-me-downs; patched
underwear, and—one of the surprises—three beautiful, sheer silk
slips, cut in a style Rita Hayworth was famous for wearing in
pin-up pictures. There were at least ten "housedresses" (that
was my mother's term for those roomy smocks which symbol-
ized for her, I imagine, a joyous acceptance of one's responsi-
bilities). There were sweaters and hats (mostly cheap ones she
never wore, for she donned the same turban-like covering
when we went for visits to the doctor's office). I wondered if

                                        Martin Tucker

she were hoarding things for the future, if she harbored secret plans of escape into a richer world, those fantasies we persist in believing capable of retrieval at the moment we savor them as towers of unattainability.

My mother revealed no confidences those last weeks when she must have known she was slipping away. (Like her daughter, she refused until the last weeks to believe it "could happen" to her.) I could not know in looking through her hoard of possessions what she thought when she bought or found them in the hallway (she was an inveterate taker of anything left in her hallway near the incinerator). Yet, as I threw things away day by day for three weeks, I was aware I was touching her identity even if she was not revealed to me.

Except—and this is always the source of our regret, the disappointment at what we did not do that we might have done—I could not help remarking how much taste her choices owned on a scale of my values. In spite of all I threw away, so many other things remained I could not let go. I had to offer them to someone, not simply consign them to oblivion. There was, for example, the horde of costume jewelry: she never tired of collecting pins and rings and bracelets, and when I was a teenager and worked in a wholesale jewelry firm I used to steal cheap objects to bring home to her—all of these, I discovered, she had kept in various drawers. Most were cheap craft but some were exquisite commonplaces, particularly a brass bracelet jangling with foreign coins (from places she had not visited) and a gold necklace with a Jewish star.

I had also planned to throw out the "knick-knacks" she kept for years in a breakfront she rarely opened. Figurines fashioned from bone china and clay, they were ornate and conspicuous of another era. Invariably when she looked at them, she sighed in a kind of yearning: they were her glass idylls. She told me they were valuable; I would appreciate them someday, she said. Looking at them now, I had no idea of their worth. Except that I knew they were not insignificant.

What they were:
> Glass jars, green, pink, blue
> Animal figures—elephants, cats, dogs
> Salt and pepper shakers, with insignias
> A porcelain red clown
> A crate of miniature orange balls from Florida

Although I knew the date, for on the first of the new month I would have to close the door on the apartment forever and turn in the keys to the management, I kept forgetting its other and holiday event: Halloween. It was a Saturday night, and that gave me an extra day to finish up the job since the management office was closed on Sunday. Looking at the remains I was not sure I would be able to finish the job even with an additional twelve to twenty-four hours. Fifteen trash bags remained to be hauled into the hallway or taken to my car (either to keep in my house or give away). I thought how like my mother I was: I could not decide on what to give away, to simply chuck out. Friends had advised me, "Keep nothing," for the deepest swamp comes when memories seep into consciousness from the feel of things in one's hand. I resolved, now, at 5 p.m., to be ruthless. In a fit of frenzy I reduced the lot to five remaining bags. Five of the huge bags and several small plastic bags of the figurines and her costume jewelry still sat beside me.

Now, at 7 P.M., I remembered the 'trick and treating" of Halloween, and thought the doorbell would probably ring, and there would be the screams of children on quest for trophies. I had never visited my mother on this holiday, but tonight I could envision the children of the buildings and its three neighboring buildings in the complex as they swarmed into hallways and pressed buzzers to their hearts' content, laughing in the high pitches of youthful sound. I was not sure if I would open the door.

I had no presents for them.

Yet there was the box of doughnuts I had bought for my dinner.

                                   Martin Tucker

And the figurines. The costume jewelry.

When the doorbell rang the first time—it was about a quarter past seven—I knew what I could and would do. I ran to the door, hoping the ringer would not leave before I got there.

He was a six-year-old, darling in his Batman costume, his mother beside him. I apologized for my lack of gifts, and then said, "I have a doughnut. Will you take a doughnut?" The boy's eyes lit up, and the mother smiled. I ran back to the kitchen and snatched the box from the top of the gas stove.

The smile the boy gave me was the widest smile I have encountered in my life. He walked away, proudly clutching the proof of his Halloween prowess.

When I closed the door I saw the bag of jewelry and the bag of figurines sitting on the floor. I knew what I would be doing next. My one regret was that the first caller would not be receiving one of my mother's gifts, those possessions I was aware she wished to share and we, her children, had derided as silly.

For these children, not inhibited by the threat of embarrassing familial assessments, would prize them. And they did. Each time the bell rang I greeted the caller with a bag of glittering jewels and shiny ornaments—polished figurines dazzling in colorful paints, and wooden, metal and glass souvenirs from far-away places. Rome, Madrid, New Orleans, Tel Aviv, London, Tangier, all mementoes I had brought back from my travels to her.

I asked the children to choose one item, to dip their hand into the bag of baubles and come up with their heart's desire. Their eyes widened as they gleaned the treasures. One came up with a miniature cup and saucer, another with a glass ballerina, still another with a soapstone seal. The ones I remember most keenly are the three girls to whom I offered my mother's three glass-blown jars—slender objects of painted glass, one pink, one green, one amber. They were not valuable in themselves, but they excited the imagination. Placed on a shelf or in the cup of a hand, each alone in spacious beauty, they created a magic.

They looked on me as a wise old man who was giving them a special gift.

I did not tell them it was they who were the givers of the gift. Or rather that it was my mother who had made the magic possible.

Other children followed through the door the next two hours. My reputation had been proclaimed in the building, and the ringing doorbell did not cease till 9 p.m. Yet cease it did, and now it was time for me to turn back to the apartment.

I thought I could hear my mother smiling in the room heaped with trash bags.

Father Works

The Missing Father

It comes back, it comes back,
     like the memory of a memory of absence
so long ago it seems of no matter I knew.
It was on a subway platform waiting for an endless train,
I said to him, "I need money."
I had been coached into it.
At ten a mother coach can be ferocious on a field
when the football is the son,
and the goal the return of the father.
In that kind of scrimmage any word will do.

He was taking me home. We had spent three hours together.
I can't remember where we went, what we did.
I know we said little in sequence, or consequence —
he might be respecting my silence, even then I thought.
Damn him for the convenience of *noblesse oblige*,
but that I would not say or ever have till now.

He disappeared long before he died,
leaving me when I was ten, which is a lie
for he came back when I was twenty-three,
all apologies.
When he returned I liked him less for coming back.
I had loved his going, not for the rightness of it
but because I felt in awe of his foe —
now she was humbled and I could take his place.
Such complexes become the building of our lives,
but a hole remains in the structure —
Those years never lived never die.

When I see a father tramping across a meadow,
sliding on a sandlot or catching the fly of a stream,
I cannot forget what is impossible for me to remember.

—2002

Martin Tucker

The Missing Father Years Before, Years Later

I see a man in a plaid flannel shirt on a subway train
and know he is my father no longer suffering and lost,
but warm.

The loss I feared for him is my loss
fed by his leaving on a winter night
and no one would talk about it for years.
A secret, and so in secret I put on a flannel shirt,
regaining his touch, and lose him again
in the wear of sleep.

Threads of such fabric never fray,
sewn in pockets no hole is big enough to lose them.

Illness

I never thought she would be jealous of my being ill,
I thought it would please her.
My mother paid her little mind when I was well.
I was ten, she thirteen. She knew the world better than I.

In hospital with pneumonia for two weeks
I received everyone's attention.
My mother went near crazy.
My sister bore the negligence. I paid the fine.

When my sister took me to a movie
three weeks later and we came out to the rain,
she sprang into the wet, taunting me to follow.
Thus began my season of unending regret

for fortunes she never received from her mother's domain.
It makes no difference to say
I was not the messenger of for-certain closures.
My pen is dipped in her ink of defiant desolation.

Scarf for Shirley

Its plaid of warm colors woven into spring,
I thought, would wake her into wading out
    on an early summer day.
Only once she said, "I'm always cold now,"
not complaining
as she fingered the scarf and returned it to me.
"Save it till I come home from the hospital,"
and she turned into the cradle of the pillow.
I took the scarf in my hand,
wrapped it in the plastic more worn than what it covered.

Amid the crowded stalls on the Rialto
I asked a Venetian lady what colors
an American lady might wear round her thin neck.
"Violet very pretty. This is new. She wear it on hot day too."
A yellow scarf astride the mauve one was cheaper
but I did not feel its touch as I led my fingers down its field.
I spoke no "troppo" nor scaled down the weight of foreign
    exchange.
Instead I assented in smile across mufti trenches of ware.
I would bring her something her hands would revel in,
some thread of hope I would needle in my mind's eye.

Memories in a waiting space:
They are wrapping the coffin in a rug gliding to ground.
The rain stays us from grasping earth for her grave.
Two months ago I brought a scarf to her bedside,
mauve-and-orange weaves to keep her warm.
"You keep it till I come home," she said.

—1982

Martin Tucker

Table Talk

Those handsome men talking about the fifties
as I looked on from an older age.
One said he had written to his sister,
advising her in a mature vein
to follow her older brother's advice and be careless.
I too write a letter to you, dear sister,
as I walk this meadow painted purple by evening.
I have no advice to give,
      and besides you were older than me,
unlike the handsome men at the table this evening.

The dead do not talk, so we talk to them instead.
I tell you of a loneliness lingering in a crowd of people,
and hear you urge me to smile in cheeks of hay.
I whisper of skinny dippings strained
through colanders of wit for local gossip,
and you laugh unrestrainedly through the sky.
The meadow slopes as I talk and you listen,
reversing the pattern when you were most alive.
I know not how to end this letter nor draw myself up
      out of the envelope of our address.
The still-living words of silence fill me with a comfort
I do not want to give up yet.

Emotion has its movement in the music of an idea.
Departing this meadow I speak in no words
      But the music you hear—
Memory lifting clouds from borders of sky.

—1982

Continuity

He went away and fathered another child.
I did not know her for sixteen years.
She arrived at my mother's door when her own mother died.
A family reunion to make the least of the past.

For years we greeted each other like pets in cages,
Refusing to touch any wires of depth,
Till her own daughter died years later
And I lifted the tax on our family bargain.

The girl she birthed had a father run away too.
So she, my niece, had a thing in common with me.
He left when she was wetting her diapers.
I upped her with a father for seven years.

The daughter's death was cruel
Not because it was slow and early
But because, at thirty-four she never had a lover,
A mad romance, or a passion beyond her mother.

Doll-like in her high and whistling voice,
Curls framing her round and pretty face,
She lipped a shy and sly smile
That afternoon in a dying hospital space.

The woman I did not call sister till then,
The child crying because she was a burden,
And I suspended all weight in a chain called hope
Because we could not lift the load of cancer.

Martin Tucker

Life has continuity most when near its end,
Or perhaps most when its end is recognized.

LIFE WORKS

Buttons

I rip buttons from appointed places.
I twist them till they come undone.
It takes days of fiddling round,
but the conclusion is a comforting sound.

Like putting on a jacket when I go to meet friends.
Nervous habit. Yet commonplace, I'm told.
But once remembering a child nine years old
in a granite courtyard slanted down a street
circling a tenement horizon—
four wooden houses chattering their cold slats
while hoarding warmth inside—
I sucked on a button I'd torn from its hole.
I wanted a sensation owning to myself,
and how, even if I would not boast of it,
I would know I had chewed a *thing*
beyond my imagination,
sucked it into caverns of my being.

I was not hungry for food that day, though we were poor,
I was angry at my mother scrubbing someone else's floor.

I drove the button down as a dare.
At archpoint it stuck in its own circumference.
I coughed, the button would not move,
My jaws jolted to an immovable foundation.
Bending I inched in air.
the button slid along my mouth.
With a whoosh and a swish I spat it out.

I felt my triumph of loss.
For one moment I held the world in my throat.
A moment later the distinction was gone,
My dominion diminished.

I wonder if my pulling at buttons,
my dare to threads in fabrics I cover myself in,
points to that courtyard scene when I was nine
and where I was king in splendor and ache.

Martin Tucker

Three

What I remember as the tent came down
was that we were about to confess our longing,
—call it desire or lust— that night on an island in the Atlantic.
We'd reached a plane of admission
we dared not enter in the neighborhood of home
as we lay in that sphere where Orville and Wilbur flew
to a sunrise of transcendence.

We were three, and darkly I wanted one.
He wanted two—his wife and me.
We'd camped in a park, not planning on groundwork.
The turning of the leaves was slow, and I, the eldest of the three,
denied what youth and freedom were whispering—
till I gleaned from my mire of ignorance—
that in a threesome one of the lovers is the greatest sharer
though he or she may be the least addressed.
It came to me that the giving of love is the opposite of possession,
a treasure lying in renewal of memory's library card.

I was unbuckling my belt for the drawing of the triangle
when the tent toppled and mocked my strategy of hesitation,
carrying the three of us into the peg of dawn's awareness.

Abdication of Guilty Evasions

I didn't give away the million I never had,
I couldn't confess to any great sin (I'm trying to find one),
I thought of donating 1,000 of the 3,000 books in my bedroom
but decided logistics were against it.
The truth is, it's hard to give up a thorn
you've worn for so long your head feels
unclothed without it.
What I did, I don't know how I did it,
I said that's enough, and suddenly it was.
Friends marveled at my new posture,
foes I've never met gazed significantly
before wandering off to bushes I was indifferent to.

In this new kingdom I don't question my fortune.
Spending it I discover I become richer.

                                                        Martin Tucker

The Richness of Poverty

I'm in love with my poverty that was,
the fullness of knowing what I did not have,
when I owned what no one could take from me.

I feel this treasury of minted memory:
The one thing I gave her, she said,
the thing I never had, he told me,
was the knowledge of poverty I gave them.
Like the cutting of a cupcake into five pieces
for a party
or the theft of napkins for a good nose job
in tissues of afternoon,
or simply going without
on an outing somewhere.

These are possessions I must throw away
If I am to grow naked and generous again.

Eugene O'Neill and His Carriage to Greatness

I've read Carlotta Oi'Neill carried Gene on her shoulders
whenever pressure wobbled him.
As soon as she saw him shaking,
she hoisted him up and brought him to bed.
Or to a stuffed chair on the patio
where she fed him hot milk or tea,
or a pill of something stronger.

After such exhaustion he breathed easier,
and she sighed more quietly.
Theirs was a marriage of connection.
He wrote his greatest plays through her nurse's aid.
She gloried in locomotion of service.

I have known strong women in my time.
None has carried me on her back
(Perhaps I've not been sick enough,
and one can't have everything—
that's not how dramatic conflict works.)
Still, I think if a woman carried me
to an armchair tattered or leather,
before I was stricken with the necessity of it,
I might rise to the occasion of something extraordinary.

                                                                    Martin Tucker

For Martha

> In Surrey Gaol, Leigh Hunt "soulfully
> disguised the barred windows with
> venetian blinds, used paint and paper
> to cover the walls with a trellis of roses
> and colored the ceiling with clouds and sky."
> —Times Literary Supplement, March 5, 2004

Leigh Hunt imprisoned for two years
because he called the Prince Regent. fat
and a libertine without concern for the body politic,
remodeled his cell, painting the ceiling cerulean blue.
Clouds of white rested on azure space
to greet him within walls he daubed bright white.
He colored the scene with a trellis of roses, a bust
of Homer, a portrait of Milton lent by a friend.

Hunt resided in confinement, asking no favors,
only paper to write articles whose print might manacle him.
Venetian blinds on his windows restored a vision
of comfort beyond the barred injustice.
Visitors marveled at gardens his mind made.
They departed with plants of his imagination.

Wardrobe of Trust

He was resting on a sofa—he would call it a chaise lounge.
Doctors had removed the lining of his heart weeks before.
He wore a blue silk negligee with a lace collar.
Ribboned sleeves clothed his thin and pale arms.
Round his neck ran a cross dependent on a silver chain.
I speculated on their friendship—had he worn these wares
          for her?
Or was he too tired to change once he agreed to her visit?
She had phoned right after her hurried breakfast.

His lover came into the room, gently puffed the pillows.
Would we like tea, or perhaps sherry? he asked.
Standing, the sick man fingered his cross.
His dress swirled all the way up to his loins.

"The dress is a case of arrested development," she said.
          "I love him still."
"His wardrobe is a design of trust. To open your eyes,"
          I replied.

Martin Tucker

At an Improv Exercise

I love you, I shouted.
The instructor was wheeling us round,
a snake or a circle as we decided,
each yielding to a soul within.
Practice your breathing, let the spirit roll,
free yourself from irons of will,
he bellowed in waves of chanting.

See not the partner, see what you see in him,
This is improv, your true self.

Following instruction, running free,
the one before me, by chance a man,
who was to be no gender but an object general.
Three times to the balding man
I love you, I cried.
My object turned away,
silent to the entreaty.

At the break and before we began again,
he disappeared. Found in the men's room,
unwilling to return to class.
I believe he believed
I meant what I said
when I was acting a part.
Or was I?

Divorce

It's losing things,
like the brown pants
I wore last spring.
They're not in the closet.
I've looked.
Or the left lens of my glasses,
it popped out, I don't know where.
I've watched TV without it,
the story frame was very good.
The next day drove to school,
something was missing
but the pupils didn't say a thing.

I keep thinking I'll find them
and she'll walk in the door.

—1980

                                    Martin Tucker

To a Young Man Experiencing His First Divorce

It's like a disease that has to choose its course,
running from top to bottom and back up again,
and then one day it backs off,
its feverish purpose done.

Memory is such a disease,
or else a journey forward.
you make it light or heavy as you please,
you seal the bag and then explode it.

I lumbered for ten years
before I put the pining in a box,
boarded up the sorrows.
There's nothing wooden about me now.

—2001

Cap du Seine

How many men can say I've put a cap on the waters?
Canute tried, but he was not a man of the tides.
More modest, I preened in my leather cap.
I had crossed a bridge in life, bought the cap
to celebrate my burgeoning powers.
I marched from the Ile de Cite in my emperor's new hat,
unaware a classless wind would lift my hat into the air
to circle the azure like a constellation
and fall in triumph to fishing waters.

Like a royal barge it sailed up and down the Seine,
Feeding fibers into the stream.

Hatless in Paris I moved beyond sorrow's stasis.
I've enriched Paris, I cried.
Can there be greater fortune than that?

—1998

                                          Martin Tucker

Edith

"This is Edith, the woman you used to sleep with."
"Yes, I recognize your voice."
"I have to ask you an important question."
"I thought we had gone all through this."
"No, this is important."
"Well, if I can answer, I'll answer it."
"Did you sleep with anybody when you slept with me?"
"Oh, Edith. You were somebody, not any body. If you mean,
     anybody else?—"
"I mean anybody else."
"No. You're asking because it's a matter of health. There's no
     danger."
"I'm asking because it's important."
"Okay. Did *you* sleep with anyone when we were sleeping
     together?"
"No."
"Good."
"Well, that's it."
"That's it."
"How are you?"
"Fine. Busy. Busy as ever."
"You've always been busy. No change there."
"No change."
"I should have a bill for all this no change you keep talking
     about"
"You said we were each to pay our way. Separate but equal."
"And now we're equal but separate."

"Yes."
"Yes."
"Goodbye."
"Goodbye."

—1996

Martin Tucker

Felt Experience

I am curious about felt experience.
Is it like the skin of an animal,
or a pelt across the face,
something you feel beyond the bone?
Unfelt experience must be more extraordinary,
I imagine,
certainly out of the ordinary
feel of things.
I used to think unless you profoundly missed it,
experience was something you felt,
the way a memory has no meaning
till you bring it back. Or forward.
So how an experience is felt
when it is already felt
baffles me.

Like waiting for a train
to reach a destination
it has passed..

—1991

War and Cease

In 1945 I was in high school gym,
The war was not over, there was a chance
I could slide into one last battle hymn.

Skinny cotton shorts covering my thighs
I dreamt of olive green fatigues
Not knowing yet how to raise a gun to my eyes.

We clapped our hands overhead,
We squatted and flipped our legs.
We were proving we could stretch across enemy beds.

I was sure I heard a sergeant barking orders,
I was sure I began marching to my locker,
To shower a sweat of manhood in my quarters.

Slipping down those stone steps
I heard a barricade of legs fall away.

When I woke I touched the blanket
Wrapped round me like a flag.
I was still in the corps, I was not out of that banquet.

You fainted. You had us worried. Are you smoking?
All true except the last.
I must have tripped, I said, joking.

They wouldn't let me drill anymore,
A weak heart, they drafted the sentence.
Before I could protest, the war shut its door.

                                          Martin Tucker

Alzheimer

What I fear each night
is what new thing
I won't remember
when I wake up
the next morning.

Always there is one more
thing I've forgotten,
one more thing
I'm trying to recall,
for some reason.

For some reason,
it comes to me,
something I cannot remember,
that's when I try to remembers
something that got lost last night.

The Ultimate Penultimate

It's not enough to say —
I like the word,
I've said that many a time,
though never said it would be the last time
I'd say it.
Aside from the salivating sound,
what makes it attractive on the tongue?
Perhaps appeal lies in a concept:
the last chance before the last mile —
dodgy terrain for wily men,
 leaving room for the surprise turn.
There's something awesome in it,
when you have a fighting chance
to turn tables round,
before you're strapped to a chair
you may even like.
Like on a stage and you're doing your act —
reading a poem, trying out a monologue,
just one more bit before the end, you say —
Honest, you claim —
and one more means one plus more,
for not till that end are you committed to end.

How delicious to think you have the time
to change the time when time is running out,
and to have two chances to calm growing restlessness,
or excite a resting urge, to bring alive a flame
whose wick soars with hope of enduring moment,
the tinder of hands rubbing to a roar.

                                        Martin Tucker

Whoever invented penultimate was extending a contract,
a one-more time before the last time,
the penultimate one always a friendly reach at hand.

—2005

DEATH WORKS

Near Times Square

They bent his leg like a doll's
before they lifted the other foot
into the zippered bag.
He fell from a window
stories untold onto the ground.
Did he jump? Was he pushed?
Or was he exercising a right to fly
on whatever high he wanted to descend?

Splayed like an embrace,
one arm cuddling a blanket on the noisy street.

When they lifted the blanked and I saw
his white tee shirt and black jeans
I wondered if he was cold that windy day.

If that was why the medics threw the blanket back over him
before they put him in the bag.

Death Be Not Lonely

And did you die alone in a room? I want to ask,
but cannot wake the dead for alarming revelations.
The news came over the transit of emails,
yet I will not phone others for unvraveling of your quickness.
You hinted at a sensational novel,
telling of plots you planned for this devotion.
Each time we met, your sad eyes
did not tear away the rush of your talk.
I'd given up on your addiction of promises
but listened to you as a fond friend of such talent
as are found in classrooms of all ages.

I do not know what lies in your bedroom.
I do not want to see manuscripts you have not written.
The tribute I pay you is not in your wasting years
but those afternoons when a day went unfinished
and being so, was all the more well-spent for it.

Martin Tucker

For a Friend of D.H. Lawrence

Making preparations for his suicide, Magnus wrote,
"I want to be buried first-class."
The police were waiting outside his door,
again to steer him onto new ports of exile.

Packed for eternities of transience,
Magnus dug paths of sanctuary everywhere.

What I cannot fathom is that desire to be buried first-class,
for after all the masquerades I would think
he would want to rest in a plot of simple content,
so in that compartment of awakening before the police
          stormed his door,
when he took strichynine or whatever poison was at hand
(only the first-class kind in his cabinet of tricks),
what determined his scrabble of last command,
"I want to be buried first-class"?

They buried him in Sicily, or was it Malta?
One forgets the place.
A pauper's grave without a name.
The sod is first-class, wonderful trodding ground.

Catwalk

For Lee and Nagesh

Sweet Mischief comes on cat's paws
Leaving no silence unheard.
A drop of a leaf too quiet for him,
More to his ear a cherished figurine
Pushed from a shelf
To carpeting by a whiskery thrust.

And was it so terrible, the loss of the object—
Just another thing in Sweet Mischief's way.
How many objects Sweet Mischief broke,
Not a houseful but at least a heap
Of dust falling from history's souvenirs.

And was it so terrible, losing the china
Or the japonned vase? A tap on Sweet Mischief
Prodded a wise spanking look:
"What's the difference, Doc?" it spoke.

And was it so terrible, having a dinner party
Minus a matching dinner plate?

He's gone now, taken by a tumor into placelets
That would not break for a sweep away.
The sweetness of his greeting, the sleekness of his fur,
The cuddle of his body between master and mistress.
The mischief he played on his sly brother cat,
Nips of his smile, burrowings of his embrace.

                    Martin Tucker

Sometimes at night in the quiet house he is heard,
Smiling away, love-biting for no reason at all.

Look! Sweet Mischief is jumping into the air!

A Cat's Life

It cost thirty dollars to put the cat away,
and fifteen to take my pants to the cleaners.
Afterwards I filled up the gas tank,
forty on the head of a nozzle—
values shaping an afternoon.

How quickly he went,
the flash of a needle pricked him into sleep without pain.
The needle brings back
    the mark of games we scored in rituals—
    pat replies we gave each other,
    the smile of his raw tongue
    even now creasing my hand.

When death comes we recognize it in the key of our lock
and go on turning doors.
I think I shall always grasp at paws
    in the scratch of a day's hand.

—1990

Martin Tucker

To Erich Maria Remarque

Reaching for a butterfly when he dies,
The soldier forsakes his machine gun.
The flight is upward beyond wormwood crumbling.
The light lifts up his eyes.

Reaching for a butterfly when he dies,
The soldier moves from his machine gun.
He looks into the sky-blue air,
The light lifts up the soldier's eyes.

Reaching for a butterfly when he dies
The soldier knows he's on to something.
The light lifts up his eyes.
The flight carries him to the butterfly.

I.O.U. Irene

Gnarled bony hands like sturdy oaks,
I thought,
Forgetting there are other ways to die.
She believed holding at bay one ravage
Offered immunity to others.
The way she fought with tempered steel
The iron rigidity of her hands
Welds me into wonder
Until I remember her welcome of another habit,
The way she would not put down smoking
When her lungs ran out of air,
Or striking a match while wearing an oxygen tube
She ignited her entire face.
She joked about the pyro-technique,
Saying I'll get rid of this old flame—
Him/it/her—
Which she did, the facial tissues returning.
But no longer the power to banish guerilla infection.
Entering the hospital, she coughed proudly,
And, with admission of no error, ended a changeless life.

Martin Tucker

An Unloved One

I never liked her. She was peculiar.
Her skin was whiter than anyone else's,
And we lived in a black neighborhood.
She coughed a lot. She kept to herself.
When I opened my mouth to speak, she fled.
Her mother too was odd, a bat in flight.
Her brother really was a phantom sight,
His hands slimy, tooth discolored, broken.

She was ten, though I couldn't care less
(or rather, being twelve, I cared to mock her).
That year I learned she died of slow lupus.
No friend attended her funeral.
The mother enrolled in a crazy house.
The brother vanished into the future.

—1985

Funereal Consequences A Long Time Ago

I plucked the fifty from my wallet,
feeling a bit of plenty in my reserves.
I was returning from elegies where I learned
Christine had been an angel of feline daring
as well as mousy mercy.

"You don't have change?" the garage man asked.
I wanted the change for an unknown occurrence
might meet me later in the day.
Still his plea moved me, since his wad contained only singles,
and my charge for the parking was twenty.
More, an act of kindness was in store after hearing of
        Christine's deeds.

Hours later I discovered I had left the fifty on his desk
and he had not reminded me of *that* bill,
though I paid the proper stapled one.
I thought of phoning the garage but flinched
at the admission of my stupidity.

The act of inquiry might involve him
in a lie, or, justifying me, a confession.
Either one would endanger his job,
were fifty dollars worth my principles?

                                        Martin Tucker

That swagger when he walked me to the ribbed wire,
unchaining the bounds through which my car would plow,
bedevils me in transitions of increasing imagery.
Revenge roars from such minute burns,
and vows of goodness flicker amid stoked flames.
Yet pictures of Christine rise from the warm dead
to enlighten me to laughter at my loss.

NATURAL WORKS

After the Storm

After the storm and the three-foot-high waters,
the body part of trees leaning on my house,
the wind grabbing me by the shoulders to bellow hello,
I see a tall bird out for a drink in the new lake,
its neck stretched as it gulps forward.
My stance of wonder sounds an alarm,
its beaded eye centers me and movement stops.

Both awash on a drenched isle,
strangers in a plot shared by no other,
I back off from the bird, though I know we are one picture—
the sun out, the damage done,
a beginning the only available story,
everything shining, our boots washed in river,
and curiosity inviting us into camaraderie.

Measures of Horizon

Three trees and a hill of green are demanding attention.
Five cats are preening in the kitchen.
The air is cool over a flowering mountain.

Even in a poem I am told something must happen.
Yet I am content to let this poem be a frame
On which to hang a scene,
An envelope without heed of season.

A violet sways in an unnoticed breeze,
And I think there is movement here—
Grass claiming its dew, the sun risen presumptuously

Something unnoticed now is noticed,
And later will be unnoticed again.
I rise in this wash of horizon,
overflowing a landscape of measure.

Martin Tucker

New York Falls

Air quickens. Clothing thickens.
Breath has a way of breathing double,
Like smoke from a welcome simmer.

Hordes of hooded sweaters swirl by,
The pace of freshness picking at their feet.

A street fair: falafel, gyros, shish kebab,
Screaming/steaming their wares,
Hawkers and boiling poets grilling the afternoon.

Corn in silver foil. The biting rhythm begins,
The season seized in kernels of color.

I journey into the subway,
Corridors tapping with sound,
Color is here too in the underground.

Coming up into the wind-dangling afternoon
Some memory persists unwashed and clean,
Persists like fever to flood my being.

The cool air stirs my bones.
Autumn glistens like a silver panel.

Autumn glistens silver to push me on.

Another Snake for D.H. Lawrence

A green snake entered the elevator as I pressed for the third floor.
I saw it in the instant of the closing door,
its lithe body shrinking against the wall,
like me, unwilling to share a meeting hall.
In truth, the snake seemed more frightened than I—
it had never been in an elevator before.

When the door opened, it exited the more speedily of us two.

Martin Tucker

Angela's Dog

She sprinted faster than the wind
as sand filmed across the screen of sky.
Seeing two birds squatting in a pool of water—
their lazy puddle beach of wet warm soil—
she chased them into flight
then curbed her body for descent
into the cold ocean of delight.
Frisking she returned to her mistress,
who wished she could jump out of her skin like that.

The three of us trotted to the car,
glad for grace of reprieve from limits.

A California Landscape

for Lee and Nagesh

Sitting in a gazebo I watch mountains carbon into copies of
        themselves.
Trees lay down arms to rest on cushions of lazy green.
I am drawn to their airs.

Below in the kitchen I hear laughter of children,
parents egging them on to make waffles on a newly gifted
        machine.
Three generations sharing displays of ambi-dexterity.
Concerns to start a laughing day.

I do not want to descend to the alive house.
I want to rest here in high coolness
and sniff anemones, purple hydrangeas.
 the sounds of their names thrilling as their sight,
identities born of blooming allusion.

A mass of brown moves me to the neighboring mountains,
rocks shouldering weathered sky of time.
A parallel of human striving.
I must pare this with my other findings.

Balance accomplished, I walk down to familiar figures.
I hear again music of a procreation table,
a family adding up to a hundred and fifty years.
I warm in this sun of human arithmetic.

                                        Martin Tucker

MADE-WORKS

Ode to a Bus Stop in Sarasota

A new wooden bench
outside a marbled library
under sun-red splendor
not a soul in sight.

I've my own book
by a novelist I've read for years.
I'm wearing extreme dark glasses
to match her obscure views.

Atop my head sits a cap
with the library logo on it,
shelter against birdshit
falling in this town's sittings.

A lazy ruler resting by his pages
I open my book empirically.
I'm an element in my element,
a thinking position at joy.

A bus pulls by,
slows to a stop.
I see for the first time
the sign—I'm in terminus territory.

The engine idles,
the fumes reach my chest.
I close the world of the novel
airily into my head.

I sight another bench.
Reaching it, I reenact the ritual.
The illusion works, the sun still shines,
the idling bus is out of my mind.

Another bus pulls in beside me,
sits behind the first bus.
Passengers disembark,
hurry to reach walking destinations.

How many buses does a street take?
In this case, four to the end of the street.
Four benches line the lines as well,
stationed for resting assignments.

Too late I come to know
these benches are not for reading,
They are for people waiting for lives
to be moved in and out of exhausting vehicles.

Still, for a score of minutes
I captured a bench of pleasured air
on a street by a white library
before buses arrived ingloriously.

                                        Martin Tucker

Lord of the Flies at the Tampa Airport

How many times I've said I'll be patient,
I'll wait to be transported to my destination.
I'll not engage like others in hysterical behavior.
The panic-stricken ones,
The angry ones,
The cowed ones who sit mumbling by,
The leadership ones who offer spare words
Unhinged by sentimentality
Or cynical practicality.
Those blue-eyes (whatever the color of their irises)
No-nonsense commanders of public instruction.
There are the little ones whose innocence of travel
Appears immense,
Whose helplessness spells danger to all nearby,
Who would run riot if not restrained by rule
(senior ones fit into this groove as well).
There are the hunters who tolerate patience
On condition it be not tested,
Who seize on a landing to unlock cell phones
To declare their codes of importance.
The intelligent ones who may be overweight like Piggy,
The ambivalent ones like Golding's Simon
Unwilling to decide between defiance and submission.
The ones caught in the melee of delay
Until finally the plane is boarded and the resolute attendant
Sweetens the air with limpid apologies
(do they really care about passenger enthusiasm in aerial
        attrition?).

Somewhere in the pattern lies fire and water—
the engine spewing sparks, the tarmac ignoring stranded
          inmates.
Order flies into triumph as the plane departs
And the jails of despair—and worse, disorder—disappear.
All is well. Banners of flight flourish again.
Until the next flight out.

                                    Martin Tucker

The New Yorker Poem

Sentenced to a *New Yorker* a day,
One hour to whittle down the pile
Grown top heavy in the bathroom
And in the bedroom
And in the living room
Where the pile has to be removed
When guests need a seat
On the floor.

He has tried for years
To catch up with the months
Of weekly deliveries,
But there have been distractions —
A job out of the house, a job in the house,
A bulb in the closet, a kitchen painting job,
Intentions repeated and vows sworn
In a style unworthy of the magazine.

His wife tells him the magazine goes, or me,
He bargains for an installment plan —
The hills to dwindle to proportional representation
Of apartment acreage.
(He has heard houses suffer the same phenomenon)

Now he is obliged to rise earlier and read the magazine,
Allowing no respite from its pages
Till his wife calls him to the breakfast table.
The pile has diminished, but his eyes are heavy
And his sense of enlightenment darker in the dawn.

He has read the stories, the poems, the articles
With wonder at their achievements.
Yet he lacks the bond of friends and family—
They have no warmth for his period pieces.

Still he has come to terms with great names,
Forgotten—or discovered—work of Nabokov, Singer.
He has come to understand, late in the subject's life,
How a sleazy operator brought Elliot Spitzer down
By a chance encounter with a prostitute,
Or hundreds of cartoons that make him laugh
When he is on the toilet seat where he is diminishing the
        magazine.

He cannot deny he is up to the job.
His marriage depends on his fortitude.
He knows he has gained his money's worth,
But pleasure has gone out as regimen has come in.

He yearns to reach the end, to turn to the latest issue
Where he can give *au courant* responses to immediacies.
Yet he cannot forgo piles of the past
Which may contain wisdom of measurement
He obsesses he cannot be ignorant about.

                                                    Martin Tucker

The New Collar

"Their collars are more attractive than anyone else's,"
I offered as a post-dinner tidbit
to a simmering conversation. The hostess's nephew
was converting from Judaism to Episcopalian,
and entering a ministry as well.
"He's gay, too," the hostess's son stoked the discussion.
"And incredibly handsome," the mother-hostess added.
"Then he must have had an Episcopalian lover," a guest
          concluded,
"and the romance went to the bad."
"Or to the good Lord," another guest injected,
preferring salvation to melancholy.
"Whichever way the romance went," the first guest replied,
"has gone, is going, goes—it's all the same,
such conversions grow from one base—
churchly passions are romances lifted out of ideal losses."
"Or debased ones," a cynic commented.
"Or exalted, if you see things as a secular Jew."
"It could be Catholic too," a humble voice added.
"Or even Episcopalian," I ended, to regain the wheel of words.

Dessert came, and we converted from speculation to memoir,
from gifts of present favor to memorable anguish
recreated in a lens of edited experience.
Still, I think of that young nephew I've never met—
golden, handsome, collared to a discipline he has been seeking—
and wonder if costume more fits an occasion
than yearning books of possible answers
or even questions remaining to be found.

It is not incredible, I come to believe,
that a cloth may uncover grounds of belief.
Or that undressing is not the way to naked belief,
but rather its enemy, the false relic at the gate.
Perhaps one needs a collar, even a boa feather,
to repel daggering doubts at one's throat.

Armor once arrayed in communion turns impregnable.

—2004

Martin Tucker

Hit Man

A job well done.
Nothing sentimental.
Just a blast
At a center
Whose disservice
Must be acknowledged.
Somewhat routine.
Like wiping a slate clean
Or rubbing a knob
On shutting a door.
After the kill
A lightness in the head,
The camaraderie of the loner.

In the end
The job defeats the man.
Only in failure
When taken in chains
Across a public page
Does the man shatter
Into the satisfaction
Of closure by exposure.
Or else he lies down
To dream on a cot
Unnoticed by himself.

—2004

A New Maud Gonne

Though stately she is,
She is no Maud Gonne.
She has not heard of her at all.
Or vaguely. In her imperious way
She ticks off subjects she does not know the core of.

Though beautiful she is,
She is no Erse queen.
She does not know Celtic lore.
Or has an interest in it. She is Jewish
But nominal. A name gives her a core.

Though worldly she is,
She is incuriously innocent.
Things she has not heard of, she no longer is interested in.
Or was. Selective,
She limits her tolerance.

I look at her Gonne-like image,
Cheekbones taut as a Yeats line.
I sympathize with the Irish poet
And understand my native madness.
She tempts with vitality.

Though disciple I am,
I know her steel of indifference.
I am a periphery of her horizon,
I cannot sway her core by reason.

—2005

          Martin Tucker

Sisters Seeking a Yeats Poem

You're not my sister,
she said, fingering her sister's straw-gray locks.
My sister's hair was golden silk,
floating in oceans of luster.
Who are you? she cried.

Her sister said nothing,
fingering her now dry hair,
imagining strands golden again.
I'm Cathy, the sister said.

You can't be Cathy with that hair,
the ashen woman replied.
My sister had hair more luscious
than European princesses' crowns.
Men bowed before her tresses.
Tell me your name, she said.

In the horizon-less room the young sister
remembered those once-dazzled crowds.
She touched her mad sister's eyes
and said, I'm no longer loved for my golden hair.

Cookie: A Poem for Her Thoughts

I'm going for a cookie, he said. I have no reason to doubt his sincerity. Maybe he has a sweet tooth. Still, it irks me that he gives priority to a cookie when a glamorous woman is talking to him. I won't go so far as to say beautiful, though I wouldn't mind if others went the distance. They used to. He certainly indicates I have some charm. I mean, he does come over to me to talk to me. I've met him six times at the club—well, maybe five—or is it four? Anyway, the point is, he sits next to me. Of course I smile—but the smile comes after he sits down. Well, I suppose I do look at him. Where else am I supposed to look? It's the entranceway. Should I look at the back door?

He could bring back a cookie. For me. Which one will he choose? Oatmeal raisin? Chocolate chip? Sometimes Henry bakes peanut butter ones. They're actually quite nice.

If he brings one back, I'm not quite sure what to say. What does one say to a cookie retrieval man? *That's very sweet of you. And the cookie is sweet too.*

Will he like that? He could be like that actor I read about today in some magazine lying about the club. So much to read and so much junk. Am I being harsh? We all have limitations. Magazine ones are fifty, two hundred pages. After that, everything's heavy-handed. Heavy weight doesn't sell. Lightweight does, stuff you can look at, admire for its good looks. Yes, it was a story about that actor Ben Stiller. Not bad-looking. Not really handsome. Angry. Oh, so much hidden, explosive anger. Nice to think about, that explosion. Like an orgasm. It floods over you. So semitic-looking, those dark brown eyes, that curly hair. Is his hair curly? Does it matter? It's simian. He has that

     Martin Tucker

monkey look. A real monkey. Monkey business with Stiller. Monkeys can be affectionate, I'm told.

Do I eat the cookie if he brings one? I have to watch my weight. I'm not twenty anymore. Only once are you at that point where you can eat anything you want, without fear of consequence. After that, a figure is dependent on the figure of your age. Stop. I'm still attractive even if I have gained some weight. Just a little. Here and there. That's life.

Is he coming back? How long does it take to pick up a cookie? Really, he has his nerve. Oh, well, he's young. Not so young. And I'm not that old. I don't have to wait around for that cookie. There's plenty of life in this oven of mine.

London

In England's lane I journey
down a high hill to the bottom
of the street where I meet
two figures sprawled in a style
Hogarth would have contemplated.
The woman in a prim rose sweater
leans against the landscaped wall,
her man lies sleeping
head over heels pinching rackety feet.
The pub a yard away barks a laughter
that carries easily in this cold land.
Only their clothes are different in this asphalt of time,
While spare trees bend kindly as ever
to cover their children's murmurings.

—1960

Martin Tucker

Bobst Library of New York University

Thirteen stories to black and white tiled floor.
I rode to the top today to see it down there.

Years ago I came through the opening door—
champagne, tuxedos, gowns and glittering tile floor.

Tonight the patron's widow is having her portrait hung
amid other notables in the exhibition hall.

Years ago partners danced across the checkerboard squares..
Young in my aerie I watched from the thirteenth floor lair.

The widow trim now in gray cloistered cloth,
like Penelope awakening threads of earlier froth.

Years ago hundreds arrived, high on elevated wishes.
The aged donor smiling behind the banquet dishes.

Fifty of us gaze now at the precious display,
ideas shelved in rare books for a transport away.

Years ago I danced with my partner, a brunette,
glittering bare shoulders miming music's net.

Older now, Ulysses might sweep in from the door
and chastise maturity for complacent ore.

Years ago beaded gowns, bare shoulders excited
Expectation. I saw adventure ignited.

The curtain now is being drawn,
The hush rises to a sigh of awe.

The portrait unveiled, the image beheld.
Honor admitted, tribute tolled.

                                    Martin Tucker

Taking the Laundry Home

Or is it bringing it home?
I never did either when I was at college.
I was a day student, and besides,
My mother was a working mother.
I washed my linen every day. Surreptitiously.

Not because I was ashamed of stains—
I wished I had some to boast about.
Maybe that's the reason I take sheets home now
From whichever place I'm in (that is, when I bring
Sheets to whichever place I go). I leave fully-handed.

I reason it's easier to use my own laundry room.
When one is traveling, one is too busy
To keep sheets of errands on one's mind.

This trip to New York was to be different:
I envisioned returning sheets to my part-time abode,
Full of newness, freshly washed.
They're still sitting in my home in Florida,
I forgot to look in that special place to carry them back.

Maybe I want to keep my New York lair naively dirty.
Analytic psychology is a blanket of such folded phases.

Subtraction

How many times have we dined together
and still he asks for separate checks.
At the first opportunity. As if to proceed further
without such commerce would threaten his empowerment.
At one stroke he sets me in a corner of singular space
While he swells to the treat of family beside him.

For years I have accepted subtraction from the general sum.
Yet something keeps missing from the arithmetic.
I want to tell him life is a sharing, a friend is not an accounting,

Martin Tucker

Dusk at the National Arts Club

Two Jews sit at a table and wonder
would I have the courage to leave my belongings behind,
my home, my *shtetl*, my sceptred isle of friends,
the ghetto that is my community?
They face each other across the table
and say, *Family is where you feel you belong.*

The two men cry, *To stay was to die*
once the house, the hut, the attic was looted,
the violation not repairable begun.
One's family held up by holdings died in Europe,
the other took option of saving nothing but name.
These are choices Jews have earned,
the two men say in a club of New York's finest,
looking at a table laden with china,
their testaments old as history.

Watching a Child Watching a Train Go By
In White River Junction, Vermont

He won't look at the menu his grandmother puts in his lap.
His eyes look at their own seeing.
What dream is he holding so fast he cannot
look away from the train
for minutes and minutes in this restaurant
in Upper Valley, Vermont?

The train has left now, nothing in sight.
The boy fiddles with his spoon.
When he looks at the menu at his parents' urging,
he sees trains carrying cargoes of cuisine.

                                    Martin Tucker

Before the Play

What I think is a beautiful boy
may be a lovely young woman
smiling beside me
in a theater waiting for the curtain to rise,
and there is still ten minutes to pass.
The voice is high for a boy
but could be a castrato's.
It's low for a woman
but not far from whiskey's Lauren Bacall.
It's Australian, the voice says,
and I think there's rich Indian blood
in the background. I ponder,
Can one so unfettered with age be sitting in an orchestra seat
wildly expensive for an afternoon?
I ask, without risk of gender,
where the body is from.
The reply is a litany
interrupted by a couple crossing our feet for their seats.
References are made to men and women
who've put the body up for house visits
(one woman on a plane extended
a flighty salutation, "come visit when you're in the States,"
and the body replied, "I did").

The body laughs, and I look again
at the brightness of the smile, the cropped hair,
the boyish chest bereft of bosom
clad in a unisex tee shirt.
The stage drama will begin in a minute

but I've not resolved the mystery.
I hear the voice say, "Mum and Dad said,
'You must come home, daughter.'"
Then she tells she's a physical trainer
who takes her gear with her everywhere
(there's little to carry beside the equipment bag,
and her social world is on another plane).
Tee-shirts, jeans, a dress skirt and that apparel of mood
stuffed in the backpack at her feet.
She hands me her card as the play begins
and all through the drama I wonder
if I've got it right—this beauty happy in her wanderings?
Is this a crossing where gender is besides the port of inquiry?

                                          Martin Tucker

ART WORKS

On Imitating Wallace Stevens' Jar
on a Hill in Tennessee

Mangrove trees scalloping my window,
The blue bay—grayblue like a patina
on a landscape photo op.
The view is harmony, yet something is missing in the idyll.
I find the link in an antique shop.
A thin circle of blue moonstone
no stouter than an envelope
standing on a base of basalt,
its being sealed in a shine
of stone on sunlight filtered,
the way bay-waves move,
overlapping white of darker depth.

But that was not my intention.

I bought the *objet* for a greater catch
than matching a color already caught,
the vase, the urn, the envelope—
whatever shiftiness the container contained—
was to change the view,
and in that slight to design anew all before it.

The recliner, the leopard-patterned armchair,
The sofa, the coffee table in milk glass,
Then the addition, the urn to shadow them in new light,
Angles and planes landing on the sill on which it sat.

Challenging the government of the room,
like a congress of geometry
charting perception of site,
all journeying from my windowsill.

                    Martin Tucker

Two Poems to Wallace Stevens

1.

The emperor of ice cream is the king of all that melts.
He is a measure of confines,
A paradigm of cool in a climate of heat.

What matter if time is scooping swirls?
There is always time in the freezer
And nothing is so cold it will not flow
When flavored by perception.

2.

The eye is in the beholder,
the beholder is in the eye.
Which is I? the emperor asks,
crunching his cone of plenty
while the world licks by.

—1970

Stone

A piece of stone
I chip at
And find a face
That is my own
Yet distant like an object
Held in hand
At arm's length
Telling me
To look,
But I cannot see
Till the shape
Overtakes me
My hand
My arm
My face
And the thing becomes
Not me
But a reflection
Beyond my telling.
A stone
The meaning of
Within the stone
And I the onlooker
Like everyone else.

Martin Tucker

The Scream of Edvard Munch

At Oslo's National Gallery

I thought it would be larger,
    but it is merely the size of a sigh of conversation.

Yet the lines above the head speak a roar
    louder than sound communicates.

What noise could shudder her head so?

Caught by this woman's misery
        I learn a scream inside one's head has no door.
            A scream inside one's head
                is an ocean without a floor.

A Late Afternoon in the Park

In Central Park watching others watch me
as an artist watches me watching him
as he draws a sketch of me,
his hands penciling down a pad.

The young are awed,
frightened by the possibility
of a naked page caressed into memory.
Men, denying interest,
freeze their hauteur of grimace,
or smile complicitly
in presumed bond of vanity.
Some chortle,
believing exhibition a sporting matter.

Women are more open,
their gaze sloping to the work
coming into view
as the artist's hand chalks his move.
And I sit for twenty minutes
watching them watch me watch the artist
who is not so much watching
as transforming his sight
into the tangibility of art.

Martin Tucker

A Workshop in New Hampshire

Look out the window and tell me what you see,
I asked in a workshop on the writing of poetry.
She was the first to respond—
          No hesitation in drafts or sighs.

She said, seeing air, this is what I see.
I interjected—synesthesia, the mixture of senses.
Metaphors perhaps, she allowed,
But I see what I see, she added immediately.

Hers was a holy cloth I could not dismiss,
Though I tried to make air of it.
I tried as well to believe
Her stubborn eyes were a disguise to thwart me.

After Giving My Own Reading

For Spaulding Gray

I have long wanted to be Spaulding Gray,
Wear a long-sleeved plaid shirt open at the neck,
Speak in a funny-sad voice,
Turn gravity into something casual,
Turn trivia into solid matter—
A navel trip to the beginning of a universe.

Stand (or in Gray's case sit) at a table,
Command attention by nailing a clip
To a sheath of papers I continually shuffle.
Like him, I want to knit wit into human cloth,
Thread wrinkled laughter into fabric of day.

Martin Tucker

SOCIAL WORK

On Knowing How Close to Oscar Wilde I Came,
Or, My Day as a Prospective Juror

What publications do you read?
the judge said peremptorily.
I said I read regularly the journal I edit,
CONFRONTATION, a review designed for credit
on the literary/intellectual scene.
Eyes broke loose at that flaming title,
red glares were handed along the room,
and the judge grasped his glasses.
Issuing dampers for the imagery
I soothed:
It's not an incendiary paper.
They interrogated:
Have you written on civil rights?
Wildly I replied, "All life is a civil rite, or wrongly done—
every fiction spread on the land
is a feather-or-down on civil rights."
My wit leapt to novel bounds
as I saw the subject in new view.
Pulling out an order form
I quoted pertinent information.
The judge ruled laughter out of order,
And the defense attorney remained stern.

Later, another rejected juror advised,
You should not have promoted your magazine.
Counter-productive, she opined.

I found out the truth Oscar Wilde discovered too late.
When we are most ourselves,
        others prefer us as strangers.

        —1993

Martin Tucker

Sunday Morning in New York

A crane has fallen across the street.
Six workers and a resident are reported dead,
dozens in hospitals lay uncertain of their future.
One woman lost in rubble where yesterday
she visited a grand apartment thinking to buy it.
Stories emerge from each floor in the tower invaded,
families moved into friends' apartments elsewhere,
or to second homes in the Hamptons or Berkshires
The wrath of God at architecture grasping irreverent height.

I look out the window. Second Avenue a thicket of lights
blinking, siren-ing, rotating like Christmas balls beckoning.
Last night I walked the forbidden block to my apartment
amid armies of firemen, police, reporters and cameras.
This morning the crane lies in the bed it's made
of mortar, cement, brick and steel and glass.

I sip my coffee and wonder if I go down to buy a paper
to read about what is happening before my eyes
will I be able to return to the bastion of my apartment?
I lack identification I live in this building.
I am visiting friends gone away for the weekend.
I cannot prove I live here when in fact I do not.
Only the doorman can vouch for me
(and we quarreled last night).

Interweaving the TV screen with my window view,
the mayor is saying this is the worst construction accident in years,
the new governor talks about blood in the streets.

I sit in the comfort of my arm chair, my TV and my underwear,
I hear a truck announcing a conveyance to dissemble the crane,
to split the steel monster into slivers littering a van.
What will be done with the remains? A skeleton
for exhibition, a geometry of show,
a thrill billed as a great killing brought to earth?

A long time ago I read a poem by Ezra Pound
in which he bemoaned the coming of World War One,
because the deaths interfered with his poetry,
scrambling his thoughts into a fog of melancholy.
A colossal ego, he put poetry before the deaths of so many.
His verse (for I am belittling him) ahead of the lives of men.
I understand now the magnitude of his torment—
To open the door is to let the catastrophe in,
to keep the door closed is torment of survivor guilt.
To rush outside is at least an act
that may rescue one from despair,.
but leading where?
Where to go, how to help,
and, most, to bravely chance
the idea one will not get back in.

                                              Martin Tucker

On Losing a Notebook
After Reading Gandhi on Non-Violence

Bryant Park was perfect. Fall pushed back though it was October.
A grove of trees leading to an understanding path
in which scenes of fancy met their nature
in a panoply of color on grass.
A yellow sky and warm blue air.
My nerves were calmed to a state of muted bliss
(a Western selfishness I learned after reading Gandhi,
who told me the state of love must be shared with the universe).

I believed Gandhi's words, I vowed I would lose my temper,
depositing it where I would gain a fullness of nothing,
a plenty gathered by the shedding of goods.

I wrote Gandhi's wisdom into a new notebook
I had bought for just such a glorious occasion

I walked to Times Square to test my new patience,
found waiting for crossings, stepping back for erratic taxis,
and the taxing nerves of pedestrians not difficult at all.
It took time, but this was Sunday afternoon,
both Eastern and Western shifts of attitude allowing me grace,
and space.
I stopped at a café, ordered oysters on the half shell, a glass of
          white wine.
I paid my bill an hour later and discovered in dipping into my
          briefcase
my new notebook was missing
with all of Gandhi's wisdom in it.

Stroking my vow of patience through a storm of feeling,
I returned to Bryant Park
.It was two hours since I left the notebook there.
In my garment of thought I believed I would find it waiting.

Should I rant? The table shone bare.

It was then I understood Gandhi's wisdom.
One does not replace loss.
One makes of experience a new experience
to welcome what has been gained by loss.

Martin Tucker

Identity

> I can exclude awareness of exile
> Till someone calls me one
> —Dennis Brutus, "Sequence for South Africa"

I do not mind the morning awakening
Till someone asks about past afternoons.
I do not have a sense of pain till someone recalls a longing
I have dug beneath a leaf of forgetting,
Or brings me to a heap of memory
Planted in still and captive fields.

I've come to know the quest of comfort
Lies not in lingering on roots of affliction,
But in a sphere of voices moving onto new pages,
And records turning from their grooves.

The Comfort of Gray

When I ponder my sea of grayness
I find myself in a world without anchor.
I've forgiven my lapses but remember my guilt
at acts I vaguely recall or some not at all.

Once I lived with brushes of black and white.
Tolerance changed my colors,
painted me onto canvases of shaded light.

I find after years of wearing this habit
I cannot alter the tailoring,
this fitting that disrobes me of final touches.

Gray has become a cloak
to weather storms I must endure,
an umbrella to keep dry those choices
thundering wrath in primary colors.

Martin Tucker

CUBA POEM ||||||||||||||||||||||||

Ten Days in Cuba, August 2001: a sequence

I am not I. I am a doubter in a land of certain sufferers. I am
in love with the baggage of my history. I savor spit and polish,
polish more than spit, but maybe spit comes first, its bubble a
froth on my cheek before I burst into awareness of where I
have not come, preferring the state of absence as reservoir for
tapping into memory's hoard of what could be future refer-
ence if I choose to exercise my many presents, those gifts of
experience I've deferred for safer moments of dangerous
illumination.

I go back to my beginning. But I have already begun. I've
told a story which isn't true. In fact it lies. In fact it is a fiction.
And not a fiction either, but a poem. A narrative in which I've
invented an I. A point of view that isn't me. You see, I'm a
moderate in a nest of Lefties. I'm a Jew who's never been to
his own *bar-mitzvah*. I'm writing an autobiography aiming at
the truth through essences lacking in nothing but particulars.

I've come with three other American writers/teachers/
businessman to Cuba to look for writers for a book we are
planning of Cuban expression. We are legitimate, *ipso facto*,
we travel without going to a third country. Last night seven
hours in terminal delay in Miami, we boarded a plane to
Havana. One woman in our quartet did not drink while we
waited—she told us she crossed that line years ago and found
imbibing in literature and religion a greater pleasure. In
consequence she was higher-minded than her three compan-
ions babbling in their excitement about the fabled island.

In the morning she and her husband set off, and my
friend, who organized the journey, and I sloped to the streets
weighted with cameras. I photographed doors—parrot green

and revolutionary red, flaunted barricades to what lay behind, temporary tatters in glory of past moldings. We scouted doors and windows for two hours, soldiers shooting their way to a city's heart. One woman, bun in her hair, a slice of bread in her lap, sat in the doorway shielding a daydream only a camera's bullet could enter.

On the second day four Americans are ascending to a window capturing Havana Bay. They sit in black and silver Art Deco. Each says *hablo espanol as* if he/she has been practicing it a thousand hours, The waitress replies a touch haughtily, a touch eagerly, *Good. What would you like to order?* She speaks in an English argot. Now she is talking of dance and theatre, And poetry. *What poetry?* I ask. She does not know a title. What do titles mean anyway? her hauteur implodes. I bow to her guile, she is performing a show, a voyage from a life she cares to forget. We are *Americanos,* exotic—perhaps she has a brother in New York, a cousin in Florida—but she does not say that line. An elegance raises her from such common ploy, tricks of the *hoi polloi.* No longer a waitress in fortress Cuba, but another Rita dancing her way to glory. Or is it me, thinking she is dreaming of us as creatures she will meet nowhere but in restaurants, whose lives take on a sheen of luxury. Perhaps that is the meaning of travel—not to learn but to dream without the intrusion of disturbing connections. I admit I am a poet as is my friend. Her eyes widen. *A real poet,* she is thinking I am thinking. Each of us promises her a book of his own. She promises nothing in return. My friend asks, "Have you ever been in love?" Ana (she has told us her name and how to spell it), replies, "I don't think so." She adds, "I have a boyfriend." My friend says sanctimoniously, for he is a recovering romantic, "I have been in love every day of my life, since I married my wife."

                                              Martin Tucker

Day 3: Hemingway's House, La Vigia, late morning.

I have seen the swimming pool
Where Ava Gardner swam naked.
It was her pal, Ernie Hemingway's house.
Why should she not shed her skin where banyan trees abound?
She needed a magic a Doc could concoct.

At the writer's shrine I think of Ava
amid the bottles on his parlor table.
Tourists cannot enter the house--
like the hordes Hemingway peopled with his pen,
we would trample his rugs to dust,
creating shredded pampas of over-wrought threads.
Instead we peer through open windows,
See his bed (Mary's side of it as well),
The kitchen table where they ate
Before he went off to work,
An old man facing the sea of his imagination.
The wooden table and chairs
(modest pieces indeed),
Walled by African tusks
Fallen into poseur frames,
And the living room: a couch
And arm chairs and the bridge of a trestle table:
Separating them to join them.
Bottles complete the ritual—
The mixing of a drink, the throat of ice singing.

What did I see when I aimed my camera
At the bottles, their dust preserved for biographers?
Pernod certainly and Bacardi—
Fernet Branca from another era,
Bitter herbs to fortify a drink.
In this color I see the lovely Ava,

Terrified by the wits of visitors
Or a bitch with a litter of condescension.
Seizing a phrase to elaborate it into a gesture,
Ava proceeds with a refill from the table to guide her.
Papa is beside her, to keep her from falling into a pool of
        despair.
If she gets silly, if she undresses,
The way she does in the swimming pool,
He will lead her to her room.
And wife Mary will take another Scotch
To wave the scene into mist.

I walk down to his boat arrayed on stilts.
I ask the guard to shoot me beside the stern item,
The old man's sea horse shipped to the world
For archetypal reproduction.
Why do I not grasp this image
And ignore the prologue to alcohol
I know well from my college head notes.

Day 4. On meeting Pablo Armando Fernandez, one
of Cuba's glorious poets

Before I walked in he embraced me.
It must have been his synthesis of view,
The way I entered the garden.
Brother, he called in a language one understands,
Kissing me on each cheek,
Declaring I was family.
In a strange city that will not leave one unattended,
I found my *amigo*.
It was not the letter of introduction sent days ago.
Such notes guarantee surety of possibility,
Not the possibility of surety.
The way he waited on the patio,

                                    Martin Tucker

To show me through the mosaic house,
Moldings and tiles of a life's vision
Never squared,
Unequal parts in equal tension.
Knowing nothing of me he surmised all,
His bonds liberated
While mine constrained.
And so brotherhood begins in rites,
Flesh of age taking a step to spirit.

Day 5. Writers Union party

When you are in a garden
You know there must be a middle way
Between the flowers and the roots.
The branches are a staff of planting.

At the fortieth anniversary of the Writers Union,
Words float in the sweet dusk.
Ambassadors are here, and writers
Raised to a pantheon of national tribute.
The splendor of nature outshines the elegance
Of crafted refreshments, polished glasses, obligatory smiles.

Day 6. Hotel Victoria

I sit under a tabled sun, a corner beside a cloud for writing.
When children jump into the pool, the spray touches my
paper. Head first, fists flying in jubilation (I learn later *jubilado*
means retirement). Five days by the pool, at four in the
afternoon, music trumpeting this is Cuba, Cuba. I am lifting
my embargo of restraint as is my friend who claims he is here
on a moving mission—to gather Cuban writers into an anthol-
ogy, and he needs my advice on dealing with them. Today we

quarreled because we had to sit in an office, and he wanted to
walk down jubilant streets. I was exposing the ash of his ideals,
dimness obscuring his romantic haze. My friend, father of
four, stepfather of three more, who talks incessantly of the need
for male bonding, has left for a hike in the mountains, up the
Sierra Maestres, to follow Fidel's steps. I have been too much
for his passionate nature in my resolute need for planned
preparation. He wants spontaneous camaraderie, he counts on
fire every day, and I have not complained, only insisted on
doing things *some* way. Reserving a room in advance of arrival.
Identifying a trip a day before the event. *I am a businessman,*
he says, *I make quick decisions, I make decisions quickly.* But
why quick when there is time to be sedulous? Time for
assuring a room awaiting the journeyman. I think he has never
outgrown a young man's dream of odyssey, *let me be free, but
have all things taken care of without bothering me.* And so we
have parted for this penultimate day.

> Male bonding suffers when trenches of crisis
> Reach over plateaus of stasis.

Wandering the hot avenues of Havana, I remember the cool
of yesterday's pool. The consent of two men channeling
brotherhood in waves of living, and pipes of siren call.

> When does spontaneity become grounds for desertion?
> Is the bureaucracy of companionship
> A match for the passion of travel?

Day 7, Havana

As I mount the steps of the holy *Capitoli,*
Cuba's shrine to gilded statehood,
I think of Jerusalem and Ozymandias and the Sinai.
All around for miles and miles the sands stretch

     Martin Tucker

But the monastery stands.
What does an atheist know in a country of churches
Where three faiths proclaim one chosen one?
Still I have been known to pray,
And even a pool has waves in a storm
Flowing with firm fluidity.
In Havana the *Capitoli* is known as the White House,
Although it is chalky gray.
Modeled on Washington's Capitol,
With resplendent dome and flowing rotundas,
And a venerable cascade of steps
(Only emperors of democracy are fit to walk those steps!).
Inside it is cool dark—a giant statue enthralls the hall,
The third largest indoor sculpture in the world.
Everywhere among the bare and tattered walls
A sense of splendor trumpets the space.
I move from a table of sand paintings
To a state chamber lined in gold.
I look up the blinding wall. I look up,
And the flowers on the ceiling stretch my sight.
Despair in any size falls to the ground,
And balconies rise everywhere.
Poverty resides outside this palace wall,
And dreams take residence in eyes of the heart.

I spy the window, and the room turns a level.
Below is the street hung with wash of clothes.
Shirts and underwear lining the windows
strung across ropes to form a peopled curtain,
What do workmen in Havana wear
when sun is shining their underwear?
Women are more discreet,
laundering sex within their closed doors.

Day 8. Song of a Young Man who has come through, From Quebec Province to Santa Clara to cut sugar cane

I stand on the windiest corner in Havana,
Easterly blast spinning my cap in carnival fashion.
I have lived in Victoria Hotel for six days,
Heard words of music beside the roar of pool water.
With fruit in plenty, roots are forgotten at their source.
Meaning becomes a sigh in the chase of wind.

We are leaving for Santiago, waiting for the taxi to take us to the bus for the Western coast, where the revolution began, where Fidel came down from the mountains, and Che ambushed a railroad train tracking it into bow-tied iron.

On the bus we sit in air-conditioned freeze, invention of modern man's need to reinvent Farenheits of misery. At a coffee stop, a young man talks in English. He thinks I am on the same journey as he. He sings his fervent song.

I come to Cuba every summer,
To work in cane fields.
I keep in shape. I keep Cuba in shape.
I contribute in my way.
I pay my fare; they give me room and board.
I work beside dreamers
Hacking away at edges of efficiency.

I am French-Canadian in a land
That has forgot its birth rights.
Quebecois is another name for Cuba,
Awareness that revolution lasts
Not by blood but in sweetness of sweat,
In growing of cane
That walks a dream
And not turns it into a rod.

                    Martin Tucker

He is not happy when I say Fidel mistreats his cane workers—
One should be allowed to be gay without raising cane. Nor is
another traveler happy when we speak–she has been talking to
my friend, who introduces her. She is an academic studying
for her Ph.D. in Santiago, I am a university professor in Long
Island. We should be *simpatico.* I listen to her topic—the
presence of voodoo power in Cuban lore. She has a thesis I
cannot get the hang of—*architecture in the subtext of iconogra-
phy, and beware of curses!* My friend is bewitched by the
tangle, but it is voodoo to me, and I turn away. Nevertheless
we make a date to meet in the Hotel Melia Santiago over a
drink to discuss the charms of dissertation.

Day 9. Santiago

Athletic young men standing torso deep in water, holding
cigarettes at the pool's edge, smoke kept at fingertip distance
from tight mouths. Clean prick men knee-deep in secret
public service. Images of Fidel this time, not Che. Not the
dirty idealist, the bourgeois kid rebel, out to ply mischief till
his dream was adulterated, and even he could not deny its
formulaic capture. Che the idealist unformed. Fidel was
different, turning defeat into victory, first time round, through
rhetoric of revolution in a military court, words forwarding an
army into enemy barracks. Fidel changed a soldier's fatigues
into vestment of the land. Che limped along, his revolution
turned into a poster long after the death of his dream.

Vulture is a Generalissimo in Cuba,
A bird eating all before him,
Gorging on garbage to diminish the domain.

In Santiago one prays to the vultures.
After such prayer what is left to dream?

Day 10. August 14, 2001

I lie naked on a massage table.
The senorita draws tension from my fingers,
My toes, easing the *mal* from my legs.
Ten days of Cuba. The tenth is ending.
I am reading a book on Che,
So many books on the bearded hero.
I think of him naked on a table tortured,
Hands bound, body immobilized—
He who cared never to stop.

    Che is a name for a creed, a belief—
    And when one cares for not caring about
    Such things, a name for a name
    Binding without need of evidence.

All history brought to this moment—
The *mal* pushed into Che on a prison table
While baby oil chains my skin.
A world dying on his dirty fingers,
His body swaddled in fatigues, baptismal cloth of revolution
And I, rising clean from the masseuse's cradle.

Later, Afternoon of Day 10

I turn on television as I pack for the journey back. State
culture bottled at bureau estate shows Cuba in glory scenes. A
photo of Che

Brooding movie-star-like
        An image of Fidel
                Grave face with rebel gleam
                A ballet scene
                (grace in a wink of pink)

Martin Tucker

Medicine for the poor
(hospital dispensation)

This is Cuba, the screen tells me.
I think, is it trying to pull a film over my eyes?

I recall crowded streets, ice cream lines at the vendor's stand,
salsa music everywhere, a proud people promenading the
Malecon.

> *We like the American people*
> We do not like the embargo
> The American government we do not understand
> *The President no. Americanos yes.*

I hear the issues again from the taxi-driver's seat. I recall
images that tell of wishes—the Santiago *correo*, a postcard
stand whirling round to show all its wares. Thirteen Che's to
one Fidel. Everywhere the same—in El Morro Castle looking
out to pristine bay, dungeons beneath the façade, a womb of
water allowing no birth of freedom, souvenir shops belittling
their monument's awesomeness. Tee-shirts, pin-struck on
sticks waving in the wind, tallying the score:

10 to 1, Che over Fidel
(plus a spare one for a marine scene).
Che the icon
Fidel the warden
Che the tribute to aspiration
Fidel reminder of order.

> Che berets
> Che posters
> Che cards
> Che notepads
> Che picture postcards
> Che picture postcards

Che portraits
> In litho
> In oil
> In charcoal
> In color
> In black/white penciling

And a stray or two of Fidel military caps.

The odds remain the same in the next aisle a store away—10 Che's with penile cigar to one woman guerilla abreast a Russian rifle.

Even in the tourist hotels the rebel Che holds victory in a rack of trophy souvenirs. Perhaps it is because one of them is still alive. The dead are always better liked because they can no longer contradict our memories of them.

Day 10. Still later, at the airport

I arrive early. Five hours to go. My friend is late, as are our other two companions, they who left Havana for a journey leftward, the wife to visit clinics and examine the Cuban system, free doctors for poor people, health on a national card. Time enough for me to reflect on what has been accomplished--an anthology of Cuban writing, a gathering of views, those by whom Che is taken for granted, without foundation in memory. We have a few pages, ten days worth. My friend will say, we have to come back.

I order a cold beer, though cold has seeped into my bones. My friend has asked, after he told his story, *What is your story?* For ten days we shared hotel rooms, a bed like army buddies, he splendid as a Bonded hero, I a more wordy pursuer of women, exalting men without telling them, denying friendship through fantasy of feared rejection. Carefully macho-like I wait for him, with this secret kernel exiling me (*why secret?* I ask in an age like this). It has been the same in

Martin Tucker

two marriages, scores of romance—flowers to keep new leaves
from blooming revelation. (Age does little to decay roots of
secrecy, and new shores become markets for curtains of old
gentility.)

I hear him saying, *This journey was meant to get to know
you, friendship is for knowing.*

And my reply, *I've told you my future plans. You insist on
knowing past ones. That is not friendship, that's gossip.*

My friend shakes his head. *Curiosity is part of friendship
when there's nothing to be gained except deeper friendship.*

He is not one for lingering words. Hemingway is his
meat, though it was I who visited the bearded hero's den.
Well, my friend stayed last night on the mountain top where
Castro honed an army of revolutionary phrases. Perhaps the spirit
of the word has come to my friend there. (It would be better for
our book if he captured the island's contemporary phases.)

My words come back to me

Remembering sites turned into history on my skin:

Yesterday the children with mothers looking at mum-
mies in the Santiago museum,

Yesterday the children looking at mummies and their
mothers in the Santiago museum.

The *Museo de Bellas Artes* in Havana opening its
newly grand halls to the Cuban people– paintings from
glorious epochs of Europe, sculpture hewn from native woods
deep in island forests,

The horses and covered wagons outside the *Capitoli*,
their Gaucho drivers in plaid shirts, Western boots, jeans and
leather faces,

The jazz concerts at noon, free to flowing streets

(One *amigo* buys me a beer, he is joyous talking to an
Americano).

I thought on my first day in this city Santiago people
are stern, the way American blacks describe Koreans. Then I
spoke to them. Once spoken to, they smile.

And my haircut for two dollars, with a dollar thrown in
for a shave. Is that why I took the plunge and removed a ten-
day indulgence, a pardon for the dare of exposure of a beard's
sensuousness? I will tell everyone how cheap the cuts were—
how I told the barber I look twenty years younger. No, THIRTY,
he said. But I will know it was not age that welcomed the
cutting, it was my return to a world I have not left.

Waiting for the plane I will wonder again
How easy it is to remain the same
In the midst of change.
Yesterday at the hotel pool amid European
Tourists stripped to their bikini's,
I had a chance to dance.
The salsa band jumped in rhythm,
A turbaned giant lady shook her hips,
Four men beside her in a tune
That brought me out of my seat
To gape at their heirloomed instruments.
One beating the drum,
Another sibilating the gourd,
The third blowing a reed,
The fourth at the organ,
Announcing commands from a stool.
Made in Paris a hundred years before,
The organ beckoned with ivory score
As the player lifted a spool dictating the afternoon's repertory.
All in white, my turbaned lady
(except for her luscious brown skin)
Fingered to my direction.
I was still in my beard then.
That was as far as I went.
The vision of the combo danced freedom,
But I did not whirl in its bath.

I snapped my camera instead.

                                              Martin Tucker

* * *

I am still waiting though I have arrived.

* * *

It is the first step must be taken.
But when one knows this,
A question remains.

How does one know the step to begin the dance?

—2003

Martin Tucker

Martin Tucker is a poet, critic, editor, short story writer, essayist, and lecturer. His first book of poems, *Homes of Locks and Mysteries*, won a prestigious Books Across the Seas Program Award from the English-Speaking Union, and was selected for the Reading Lists of the New York City Public School system. He has published poems, reviews, essays and stories in *The New York Times Book Review, The Nation, The New Republic, Boulevard, The Commonweal, Research in African Literatures, Chicago Review,* and elsewhere. He has edited more than 20 volumes of literary encyclopedia.

Now Professor Emeritus of Long Island University, he lectures round the country on literary matters. He was a member of the Executive Board of PEN American Center for more than 20 years and served for two terms on the Governing Board of Poetry Society of America.

He is the editor of the prize-winning literary journal *Confrontation.*

This is his fourth collection of poems.

Printed in the United States
135109LV00004B/3/P